BURNING
SUGAR

BURNING SUGAR

poems

cicely belle blain

BOOKS

AN IMPRINT OF
ARSENAL PULP PRESS
VANCOUVER

VS. BOOKS is an imprint of
ARSENAL PULP PRESS
Suite 202 – 211 East Georgia St.
Vancouver, BC V6A 1Z6
Canada
arsenalpulp.com

The publisher gratefully acknowledges the support of the Canada Council for the Arts and the British Columbia Arts Council for its publishing program, and the Government of Canada, and the Government of British Columbia (through the Book Publishing Tax Credit Program), for its publishing activities.

Arsenal Pulp Press acknowledges the xʷməθkʷəy̓əm (Musqueam), Sḵwx̱wú7mesh (Squamish), and səl̓ilwətaʔɬ (Tsleil-Waututh) Nations, custodians of the traditional, ancestral, and unceded territories where our office is located. We pay respect to their histories, traditions, and continuous living cultures and commit to accountability, respectful relations, and friendship.

Every effort has been made to contact copyright holders of material reproduced in this book. We would be pleased to rectify any omissions in subsequent editions should they be drawn to our attention.

Cover and text design by Jazmin Welch
Cover art by Sacrée Frangine
Edited by Vivek Shraya
Copy edited by Shirarose Wilensky
Proofread by Alison Strobel

Printed and bound in Canada

Library and Archives Canada Cataloguing in Publication:
Title: Burning sugar : poems / Cicely Belle Blain.
Names: Blain, Cicely Belle, 1993– author.
Identifiers: Canadiana (print) 20200206575 | Canadiana (ebook) 20200206583 |
    ISBN 9781551528250 (softcover) | ISBN 9781551528267 (HTML)
Classification: LCC PS8603.I299 B87 2020 | DDC C811/.6—dc2

For Mum & Nana,
thank you for showing me the world
and filling it with love.

And for Peter Wanyenya,
the greatest guiding light
Rest in Power.

Contents

PLACE

ART

CHILD

PLACE

MANITOBA

I found Black people between groves of wheat

drove hours along open road back to Winnipeg

heard whispers in the topography

Ta-Nehisi said I could go anywhere

he told me in two hundred pages that Black folks could travel

said seeing the world is not a luxury

reserved for white men

we do travel though

some of us are still

on ships

NORTHERN CALIFORNIA

to be warm is to be held

soft hands touching under unblossomed orange trees in Northern California

sticky grass sweet air: tight and close but not choking

lurching on the precipice of discomfort

playing with fire

will we fall? will we burn?

will our hearts be ignited like kindling on winter evenings in childhoods far from here?

we sing the diaspora song: an aching melody

on the white peaks of Atlantic waves

crashing crescendo

each note a drop of blood on the hands of white men

always washed away with the same salt that chokes us

grates away remnants of their crimes, so too does it erase us

black and brown and yellow and red

suddenly monochrome camouflage invisible

serpentine languages of our ancestors just daggers on our tongues

bullets in our souls

we are nothing more than shells trying to fill ourselves with meaning

tears, salty like the waters that brought us here

ships passing in the night we once were

now we are docked together, anchored to land that is not ours, nor theirs

wolves, bears, thunderbirds

stars are dying, but we are reborn.

far from home, sticky grass, sweet air, tongues, tongues,

tongues of our ancestors reincarnated in us in ways we could never imagine, never deserve

but here we are, in Northern California, blossoming like fruits

finding ourselves and loving and forging friendships and hurting together.

here we are

you may have broken us, severed us from old warmths

but here we rise eternally.

DALLAS

I keep coming back to you
I just don't know what to say
never felt so much burning grief radiating joy explode upwards from sidewalks

a sign read, *Cop Appreciation Day*
I felt all of us become smaller
I felt hearts bleed songs of yearning
like I was being buried alive
there aren't words for a feeling of insignificance
we don't matter here.

I crashed a funeral
accidentally
I mourned a thousand deaths

I felt cotton beneath my bare toes

HOMESTEAD, FLORIDA

I

Back waters

swamp, stink, stuck.

heartache buried alive

snake pattern claw tooth jugular

she told me what happened here

I started putting sugar in my tea

it's a triangle that tastes like sweat

ocean waves that taste like piss

a Great Dane put his paws on my shoulders

I saw underground railroads in his eyes

mosquitos, fireflies, zaps.

this state is full of swimming pools,

littered with white towels

and acid

breeze, tsunami.

worlds end and begin here,

moonlight pledges to water at night

You are full of unrequited endings.

II

banana, mango, lychee

twelve years later.
Irma has been and gone
glorious groves lie broken in her wake

there's tension between rednecks and Cubans
the air smells like gasoline and mangosteen

HOLLYWOOD, FLORIDA

My grandmother tells stories of friendship:

1950s Spanish love affairs
red wine lips
calloused thumb hitchhiking
terra cotta rooftops
books unfinished
post-war joy and heartache
African sunrise
freedom that tastes like lust

Jeopardy! plays in front of TV dinners and whiskey on ice
aching limbs and tarpaulin skin
crook'd backs, rosacea, joints unhinged

Sixty years of chosen family rests between these aging bodies
the air is of salt and unending sunsets

I'm cross-legged on the couch
dreaming of gratitude and cross-Atlantic love

MINNESOTA

Black bodies against snow
radiating
kente cloth wears thin over broken bones
snow, sun, dancing
vibrant diaspora calls me home
Africa lives between the snowflakes
icicles drip in tongues

We took a shuttle to Target
I'd never been there before
or since
it was red and phallic in the icy wilderness

I shouldn't have followed him
but femmes are made to believe that men will keep us warm

SAINT PAUL

I drink coffee

it tastes bitter like gasoline on the Hudson River

I walk on glass bridges

my shoes vibrating with angst

I plan vigils in my mind

three years later, Philando Castile will die here

DEAR PHILANDO CASTILE

~~You're a heartbreaker.~~

~~Not the Hershey's-Kisses-rose-petal-down-on-one-knee kind. More the America-watched-you-die kind. More the my-heart-literally-broke kind ...~~

I came back to this letter so many times. I think there was so much I wanted to say, but each time I saw your name at the top of the page all I could think of was the way your blood seeped so suddenly and so swiftly from your gunshot wounds. All I could think of was the little girl in the back seat, the screaming mother by your side, the police officer frozen stiff in white guilt and self-actualized fear. All I could think about was his rapid fires. *Bang bang bang bang bang bang bang.* No hesitation.

All I could think about is that maybe he came there to kill you. In fact, I can say with certainty that he did—that all of this is a jigsaw puzzle where the pieces add up to your demise. And Alton's. And Trayvon's. And Mike's.

And mine.

All I could think about was this: How many white people can say their death will end up on YouTube? Nestled between Ariana Grande and reruns of Ellen.

I watch it. I watch you. Calmly explain you're licensed to carry. Gently reach for your ID card. Fall back, skin broken open, crimson washing over your crisp white shirt. Die. I watch you die. Over and over and over again. I read the comments. And I watch it again. Soon it starts to come on autoplay, or be suggested based on my history. Soon Facebook is showing me police academy ads thanks to some fucked-up and terribly confused algorithm.

"I've edited together the dashcam footage and the girlfriend's livestream," says one spunky YouTuber.

The line between traumatized and desensitized rushes up at me—like when you fall off a swing and watch the grass zoom in on your face.

All I could think about was traffic stops.
Broken tail lights.
Unpaid insurance.
Fatal misdemeanours.

Red and blue lights in my rear-view mirror will always remind me of you.
Red and blue lights in my rear-view mirror will always make my heart shake.

Yours always,
CB

BANJUL

I

Aunty Vicky's living room is ancestral chambers
time and history swallowed whole by Saharan dust
my grandfather looks at me through faded eyes
they told me he left for work one day and never returned
they tell me stories of a man they knew through blood and beating heart

I know him only through glass

he grew mangoes in his garden
he laminated pictures of himself
in business suits and military uniform
a typical Leo

I'm two floors above desert track and unpaved road
a sweet baby girl in hijab reaches up to me
inviting me to mosque
but I'm too high up, too far to reach her midnight hands, coated in sweet mango juice

II

Roads here are made of sand too soft for my hardened footfall

I grew up in your womb,

without ever having set foot on your desert soil

in you, I am

u n e a r t h e d

III

They tell me
my grandfather's house was amber and terra cotta walls
a thousand rough waves south of my bornplace of grey and asphalt

something about this place feels like eternal sunshine
like yellow ochre and safety

Gambian nights are hot and cold sweat
feverish fits, paradigm shifts

I saw a figure of light and dark in my dreams

الأنبياء في الإسلام

He offered me a mango
I felt the juice between my fingers, yellow and pungent
thick and binding; my fingers stuck together and became spades
I dug myself a grave
to lie beside you, in the ancestral plane

Black cats hang from mango trees there

SERREKUNDA

I

They told me I am born of royal blood
gold thread is sewn into the seams of our ancestry
my forefathers were princes and
my foremothers
they were queens

They served me a platter of mangoes;
they were made of aortas and heartstrings
splendid and aching

In England, mangoes are small, soggy, unripe
it's almost as if ~~we~~ they were never meant to be there

I miss the mangoes he grew in his backyard
the mangoes I never ate
I imagine they taste like freedom dreams love warmth

I took a boat to Canada
in 1800 and in two thousand and twelve and today
knee-deep in the golden blood of my ancestors

Mango stones ebb in the wreck of slave ships

II

They told me the monkey park was bought by Chinese investors

lateral violence sprouts from neocolonialism

BIJILO, THE GAMBIA

rapture

        is

           carefree

black boys

   endless

in   blue

    ocean

LONDON

I

some towers are made of cladding
some made of ivory

some burn in the night
some built by slaves

wind rushes through coarse hair
body aches between vertebrae
you are my first and everlasting love

you are a grey block grey sky wonder
you are the hardest poem I've ever written

II

my words are heavy rocks in my throat
perhaps there is no way to describe the
mother-daughter
abuser-survivor
teacher-student
long-lost-friend
pen-pal
relationship that we have

III

I imagine hard lines when I think of you
the beginnings of destruction
worlds upended to bring you gold

you are the birthplace of endings

gunpowder
sapphires
concrete poured over bloodstains
petrichor

I am a product of white man and Mama Africa
my bones are made yellow through violence
and time
and migration

IV

you are sharp edges

you are a city that smells like death

you put my grandparents on ships sent them back to stolen islands

you are deep, intrinsic love

you are the only world I needed.

LLANTWIT MAJOR

a black girl told me she was raped

the words burst out of her like bullets
the shell casings littered dewy mornings

my tongue was canon weight in my mouth

I wanted to tell you everything, black girl
I wanted to tell you: you *are* everything

black girl,
you are wonder made real, magic embodied; you are mountains moved by melanin
black girl,
you are luminous sunrise, sweet siren, soft silk-skinned survivor

I wanted to tell you this

but my tongue was
dead weight
in my mouth

OAKLAND

I

the joy here tastes like cherries;
it's full of slumber and acidity and wanting
in between we will mourn black boys
the sunsets they will never see
our days are hard but it is harder still to be a mother whose womb aches just sixteen
years after it made magic and cells to form you
"Don't go that way, it's sketchy," the white lady said
pizza came through a divider
cops circled the block like American eagles
the street corners were fiestas hospitals schools all at once

how can I not feel the burn in my fingertips when my family tread fire to feed small mouths?
how can I breathe when they can't?

Canadian air is too fresh for a scorched throat
Canadian water is too pure for a tarnished body

my heart is a crater of guilt

II

our ancestors' violated bodies rest on our backs

intergenerational trauma becomes guilt

three glasses of wine each night, skinny blades on dark skin,

wake, sleep, move body

spaces become toxic with other people's guilt and shame

we absorb each other, never digesting, only meeting sluggish eyes over glasses filled with

pain that is our own and entirely not our own

we are sorry, but we are cowards.

NORTH CAROLINA

heat stretches out for miles

fields, brown and crackling

I can feel the vibration of mosquitos in my veins

it's my first time in the South

they laughed when I asked, "what the heck is grits?"

my body gravitates towards the magnolia tree

it has always been my favourite

pale yellow flowers reach upwards, undoing gravity

I am in the shade of the tree before I see it

the whipping post

stands short and unassuming

I am almost disappointed by how dull it is

a piece of wood, struck jarringly into the earth

a slight eastward disposition

I expected inflictions of time

deep wounds of history

blood of my ancestors

a haunting chill

pain in my own fragmented heart
the smell of burning sugar

instead it stands there
in all its regularity and reticence
with no stories to share

as if all the violence of white supremacy
would simply fade with time

CACHE CREEK

We took a wrong turning and ended up in you

the air smelled like violence

I can trace the journey of white men by the trail of never-meant-to-be asphalt

a rock lodged itself under my car

these are lands resisting colonization

I felt pieces of my Toyota Yaris become unstuck

Pangaea becoming continents

this was the earth reminding us of some 150 years prior

there is too much grief in trying to live

knowing, in our bodies,

we were never meant to be here

ALEXANDRA BRIDGE

I

all this metal and stone does not belong between the aching labia of this creek

just as I do not belong between your satiating lips

forgive me

II

I rediscovered friendship

I twisted my ankle falling into Earth's core

I forgot you could be loved like this

III

the hardest part about decolonization:

even the air we breathe has been colonized

PENTICTON

I

the farmers' market reminds me of humans trying to be humans

it reminds me that we have all been colonized

II

a big white man

selling vintage toy cars

shouts at a young Asian woman

a jolt in my body

my heart, exalting

my body primed for flight fight freeze flounder

he is exposed

a veneer of pleasantry/normalcy/acquiescence

C R A C K S

to reveal his truth

the history of racial tension baked into his bones

primed him for this moment

maybe—he didn't even know

(most of the time they don't)

what waited inside him

stories from his ancestors

notes from his father's unwritten memoir

maybe—he's just a carrier, a conduit

yet there it was

visible to the trained eye—mine

a biological desire to

other

intern

enslave

displace

PEACHLAND

I didn't find a single peach
and I'm fucking pissed tbh

LÉZIGNAN-CORBIÈRRES

I

You were a soft-petal landing for my trauma.

Nazis were chasing me in my dreams and down Granville Street.

I didn't know I needed you
until you gave me crusted dough and brie at sunrise over thatched roofs and cobbled lanes

fourteen years ago, a few cities west of here
I cried burgeoning tears
queerness rooted itself in my chest
throbbing against the membranes of my body

II

There were six people in my village

I grew up on MSN
catfishing myself into straightness

you don't know loneliness until you are the only black gay kid for a million miles
I became friends with trauma
to know my worth

III

I'm back now

the brightest nebula of self-love I've ever been

I rise early to watch faint orange stardust on the horizon

you wouldn't believe the places I've been

some days, I considered darkness

then I remembered you,

soft cheese

big prawns sautéed on campfires

baguettes, long like painful memories

cobbled streets

canals to nowhere

beautiful agony

love, undone

uprooted flowers

salt lakes

my mother, resplendent.

VANCOUVER

I've never been asked
so many times
if I'm the help.

METCHOSIN

I

You are wooden like I've never seen before
timber the colours of sunset

the first time I saw thick logs floating on the Fraser River
they looked like history
time
the end of the world

I learned about deforestation in high school
I didn't know trees held families
in the ache of their sap

I didn't know trees were medicine
I didn't know trees were life

who are we to build shelter in someone else's skin

II

I hate routine
but this yearly haunt brings nurture to my waning bones

CHILLIWACK

It's just a Walmart.

SALT SPRING ISLAND

I lie on prickling grass
fingers entwined with my best friend's
sun bursting through the pores of my skin

we roost in each other's joy
tipsy on sugar and rage
sisters from the same Mother Land

a dry and radiant sun, market buzz, the slap of woven sandals
distant sizzle of spiced meat, humans meandering, small waves beating rock

dreams of liberation
flit across our tongues

with our eyes closed we could be elsewhere
where we're supposed to be
where our hearts were born

abruptly,
"Get off my land"
shouts a white man

TORONTO

It's 3 a.m. I'm sitting on a balcony at the corner of Dundas and Gladstone—the neighbours are playing late '80s alt rock, and the air smells like smoke and chocolate. My rainbow platform sandals, half a joint and a flag striped pink-white-blue lie around me like an altar to my queer liberation. Marsha P. Johnson is pinned in enamel to my lapel—brown skin and flower crown immortalized on my chest. A wind blows the pages of the Toronto *Pride Guide* open and closed like an accordion—rainbows, glitter and unicorns practically exalt from the pages. I'm not usually that kind of queer, but tonight I am.

———

I often think about my relationship with fight or flight. Am I more likely to attack—run headfirst into conflict? Or will I flee, taking any opportunity to escape my fears? Perhaps both, I've concluded now.

When things become *too much*, my first thought is escape. My browser is thirty flight-search tabs wide, my suitcase is never quite unpacked and my passport doesn't live in a safe or secure hideaway but on the bookshelf along with my other prized and well-read books. For many nights, my cursor will hover over the "Book" button, but it will be months before I click it.

Instead, without even really thinking about it, I'll fight. I will get up every morning with the weight of injustice in my body, and I will resist. Mostly in small ways—by picking out my afro for a corporate meeting or by correcting someone misgendering a friend or by speaking my Wolof ancestors into a space or by secretly ripping a pair of Lululemons in the fitting room because my ass is too big for their size 14.

Then in big ways, too—raging through the streets, screaming, chanting, standing face-to-face with armed police officers. I rage online, too—exposing, questioning, educating, moving us marginally towards liberation. On any given day half my brain capacity is planning vigils, writing speeches, crafting the revolution.

I do fight—in ways I've told myself are not enough. Not enough because I carry a sort of survivor's guilt. Not enough because my ancestors gave me a freedom I'm not quite sure how to use. Not enough because I am hopeless, inevitably, against thousands of years of systemic oppression. Yet, most notably, my brain says, *Not enough* because I am not enough.

When all this is done—and nothing has changed—I'm ready for flight. Suddenly, and desperately, I must get out. Vancouver becomes suffocating—the mountains seem to close in and the ocean's endlessness is more daunting than beautiful.

I am so primed for these inevitable departures that I live on liquids less than 100 mls in quantity and own more bathing suits than underwear. Travel, my greatest privilege, becomes my greatest escape, each trip shadowed by guilt and conflict.

———

I'm nursing a bruise on my left knee—the rainbow platform sandals got the better of me. My body aches with exhilaration, my toes twitching with memories of the dance floor. The city is a euphony, but my ears still hear the microphone-distorted chants of *The face, the nose, the teeth, the eyes, the structure!* and *Tens, tens, tens across the board!*

This is my seventh year as an openly queer person—and the first time I've enjoyed Pride. Toronto Pride engulfed me with as much ancestral power and depth as a glacial lake—in love, in community, in liberation, in Blackness but most importantly in anonymity.

I felt what I have always desired and, I think, despite the ridiculous rainbowy spectacle, what so many queers want to feel—invisible. I was just another rainbow-clad, brown-skinned, tattooed femme, swaying off-rhythm to scratchy megaphone music.

We walked and walked, until my Fitbit thought she'd been stolen, and arrived at a park. So much of Toronto looks like London, and this low-shrubbed, litter-strewn green enclave was no different. I felt simultaneously at home and washed up on a foreign shore. Drums were beating in a way that, despite my amusic tendencies and painfully limited connection to any non-Western culture, somehow felt universal and intimate all at once.

Back on the balcony, I still feel the rhythm rushing through me, and momentarily, I'm called to consider queerness my religion.

———

For years, I experienced seasonal depression. Winters were a blur—Halloween, my birthday, Christmas became almost ritualistic attempts at finding joy, at finding reasons to live, at finding feeling. My excitement was performative—an attempt to convince mainly myself that life was worth living during those dark and rainy months.

Summer was a relief. English Bay became solace, evening walks along West 4th were simple and sweet, cabin trips were consolation and Kits Pool at 7 a.m. was unperforated bliss. Summer provided all the answers winter sought, and for a long time I lived in this binary.

But as quickly as I found freedom in coming out, it was snatched away from me by white supremacy. That's when summers became unsafe. My first gay summer—like those of many young queers—was a mess of asymmetrical haircuts, plaid shirts and unrequited crushes. My second gay summer—like those of so few others I knew—was a painful, lonely existence. A kind of loneliness that was not new to me; in fact, it was all too fucking familiar.

It was the same loneliness I felt in chat forums in my early teens—posing as a boy to talk to girls, I soon realized it wasn't enough for my alter ego to change genders: he had to be white, too.

It was the same loneliness I felt in ninth grade when my best friend came out and something—her whiteness, I now realize—made it possible for her and not me.

The same narrative always followed me and continued to tell me the same lie: Blackness and queerness are not compatible.

Queer people are white. Queer bodies are thin. Queer bodies are masculine. Queer fashion is Western. Queer people are white. Queer people are extroverts. Queer community is sex and vodka. Queer desire is some variation of the L Word, *where you don't even know the Black one is Black until you google her. Queer people are white.*

Then, one night, I dreamt of a march for Black, queer liberation, right through the centre of Vancouver's (cis, white) gay village. I am not a particularly spiritual person, but I know when I've had a dream that is less an imaginary trip and more an undeniable call to action. My co-conspirators believed me, felt their own calling through mine.

In 2016, my friends—my family—and I began what would become the hardest yet most transformative journey of our political lives. We stood at the foothills of Davie Street; she seemed dormant, unexpecting, pressing snooze on liberation. Rainbow flags fluttered limply in the summer breeze, and despite being in the heart of downtown, the air felt like slumber.

Until we marched.

The street awoke with the clang of our resilience ricocheting off the blank stares and raised eyebrows. *They stared, we marched, they stared, we marched.*

The rainbow crosswalk lay waiting for us, simultaneously bright and dull, unprepared for the arrival of our Black bodies. We lay down, our limbs splayed, deformed from the centuries of violence rippling in our skin. We had the phone number of a lawyer written on our bodies— the permanent ink stayed for days as a reminder of how unsafe we are. Comrades drew white chalk outlines around us, leaving evidence of a million unsolved crimes.

Sisi Thibert

Alloura Wells

Mesha Caldwell

Kenneth Bostick

Ebony Morgan

Ava Le'Ray Barrin

Keisha Wells

Diamond Stephens

Muhlaysia Booker

Michelle "Tamika" Washington

Jazzaline Ware

Dana Martin

I hadn't prepared myself for the feeling of my body against the burning tarmac, the eyes of the thousand-strong crowd, my heart pounding against my chest. It was simultaneously political resistance and performance art: our Black bodies strewn across the intersection, flanked by rainbow flags that had forgotten what they were. It was both jarring and completely normal to be Black and queer and dead, in the middle of the street.

We asked for recognition, safety, compassion, empathy and freedom. What we got was dismissal, hypervisibility, vilification and violence.

———

The morning after Toronto Pride, my body lethargic from alcohol and tears, I boarded the train to Montreal. As Toronto disappeared behind trees that BC forests would call small, my heart felt dizzyingly full. I sat in this pleasure as the train sped through parts of Canada I'd never seen before; time felt suspended as the green views blurred into one. I shifted in and out of consciousness, half dreaming, half remembering the way sunshine and safety felt on my skin.

A news notification popped up on my phone.

BREAKING: EIGHTEENTH TRANS WOMAN KILLED THIS YEAR.

ART

SOUL OF A NATION

Tate Modern, London, United Kingdom

Inside the whitest walls, my mother and I found *Soul of a Nation*—an exhibition dedicated to the American civil rights movement and all the dreams that rose and fell with it. The exhibition begins in 1963—a year full of strife, anti-Blackness and state-sanctioned violence. Artists design a blueprint for revolution; sculpture, painting, drawing, film, text scream for justice. A desperate cry for liberation aches from canvases.

The art is American in the deepest sense but also African. Mouhammad Ali, Jack Johnson, Angela Davis, Martin Luther King Jr. and Malcolm X dance from white plinths. The juxtaposition is nauseating. The stories of Black pain carve irreversible lines onto my heart. There is love, too, though, scattered like Ben-Day dots through the exhibition. Sometimes joy, rippling in brush strokes, occasionally hope and always resilience.

We look back at a history that mirrors the present with such accuracy that sometimes I double-check my phone for the date.

Having an artist for a mother means many a weekend trawling the galleries of Europe—item #2378 on my list of things-I-now-realize-are-a-privilege-but-disliked-as-a-child. The Tate Modern is a staple in the diet of artists' offspring. She stands tall and ugly on the banks of the River Thames.

Sometimes I think the air around her smells sickly sweet: a mixture of the sugar and blood money that built her.

I want to believe that exhibitions like *Soul of a Nation* represent a revolution. Black vibrancy against white walls, inside brick funded by slavery, on land used for incarceration.

What if this is just oppression disguised?

SISTER, YELLOW

I

there are so many of us here
by *us*, I mean kin
Black bodies held close by winter
crochet, to keep our African bones warm
broken kinks of blackbrown
coarse, bending towards spring

thanks for your trauma
it holds us
she's wearing a yellow sweater and denim shorts

II

they talk loudly while we cry
some are posing
what will they do with the selfies they take on your dead body?
is there a filter for white guilt?

I HATE WHITE PEOPLE IN ART GALLERIES

I

a white man blocks my view of your work, Archibald.

the irony has you reincarnated; we're in the graveyard of liberation

you never painted again. you bled on that canvas.

he photographed your blood

I blocked him with my body

he tutted white middle-class frustration

my palms bled

I swear the devil is in chinos and Birkenstocks

I wanted to rip your painting down

I needed to un-lynch the canvas

white peaks ebbed in the corner of my eye

I stood my ground

it was the least I could do, ancestor

I am eaten whole by your expansiveness

swallowed into rich earth

the blinding whiteness of the art gallery still burns through black soil

cocked heads

blond hairs

gold-rimmed spectacles

headphones so they can listen to a soft-voiced white person explain the meaning of the art

kale snacks

man buns

private school field trips

they'll never know the pain you etched here

they'll never even try

II

intergenerational trauma manifests as survivor's guilt

I want justice

also, I want vengeance

LISTENING TO TRACY CHAPMAN WHILE OBSERVING ART

there is no gender here
we are wives only to each other

STOP KILLING BLACK BOYS

childhood was asking what we wanted for our birthdays
now we are happy we made it this far
do you raise a black son having already planned his funeral?
they nursed your babies. you kill theirs.
the history of America
there is gold on the horizon, but you'll have us mine it
from the wombs of our own mothers

DEAR MARTIN

Am I really a Black activist if I don't write to you?

Am I really a Black activist if I don't believe in your Dream?

Am I really a Black activist if I am not moved by your words?

Am I really a Black activist if I don't quote you every February?

Am I really a Black activist if I don't have a shirt with your face on it?

Am I really a Black activist if I don't agree with your nationalism?

Am I really a Black activist if I believe your flaws outweigh your good?

Am I really a Black activist if I'm not sold on your commitments?

Am I really a Black activist if I speak ill of your name?

Am I really a Black activist if I wanted more from you?

Yours always,

CB

DARK

white on canvas, black
how can small lines give me chills?

this is why we are scared of the dark
whiteness lives there

DEAR ARCHIBALD MOTLEY JR.

Today, the sun is shining.

If I close my eyes, I can almost feel the melanin shifting on my skin—writhing with angst as it replenishes after a hard winter. I wonder if you ever experienced a Canadian winter: a piercing, unkind winter. Sometimes I imagine Harriet arriving here; I don't think anything can prepare a dark, African body for the whiteness of the North.

I'm writing because I've had another one of those days. You know the ones? The ones so deeply rigged with anti-Blackness that you forget we're not shackled anymore. The ones so shadowed by white supremacy that Africa seems like another planet. The ones so steeped in racial prejudice that freedom, emancipation, independence seem like conspiracy theories.

You validate me—the way you painted Blackness so vibrantly, so diversely. You painted Black people who were burnt umber and yellow ochre and midnight blue. You made it seem so effortless, like refracting light is as easy as cracking an egg—like translating the rainbow to all the hues of Black and brown is as simple as making breakfast to you. I'll have my Black liberation with a side of hash browns, please.

You wanted white people to see us as individuals. You wanted to undo centuries of dehumanization. You took on an impossible task. You see, they don't see nuance. They don't see complexity. They see Black. And they see white. And they see violence.

Here we are, you and me—mixed race, mixed up. Our skin like oil pastel smudges of our varied ancestors. Are we Black? Are we mulatto? Are we half-caste? In the end, it doesn't matter. We are slaves.

I think of your final painting a lot. I know the exact moment, the exact feeling of darkness that overtook you. It's like the day an apple switches from ripe to bad, and it cannot be undone.

Archibald, you spent your career painting jazz concerts and worship and spirited community. The formations of those Black bodies you inked exuded joy and defied logic with their undulating curves. It was as if you inhaled the resplendence of melaninated bodies in motion—and breathed them out onto canvas. I can almost see the urgency of Black celebration dancing from your brush, like I can see the breath leave my mouth on a Canadian winter's day.

Then it all stopped. Abrupt, like a chained dog running, only to be pulled back by its leash. I can almost feel that yelp of confusion, anguish, betrayal.

Freedom is a lie.

I don't need to ask what happened, because I already know. I already know that feeling of heartbreak, greater than the breakup of any monogamous relationship I've ever had. Worse than that—more like a tectonic ache, a seismic shudder, ripping seams down your fragile skin. It's the moment you realize that no matter the year, no matter the postcode ... anti-Blackness is unending.

You painted the colour of pain, the colour of battles un-won, the colour of grief. Artists change their styles all the time, I'm sure, but never is their anguish so visible as yours. Never do their canvases smell so violently of destitution. Most notably, and most sadly, I think you painted the colour of giving up.

I'm sure it took you years to paint that final painting, that fateful graveyard image. A graveyard of attempts at Black liberation, watched over by the Confederate flag. King's head hanging from a noose, white-peaked gowns in triumph, policemen with dogs. The First One Hundred Years, you called it. One hundred years after they claimed they set us free. And yet there is still the clanging of metal on metal as you lift your hands to paint.

No wonder thirteen is an unlucky number.

I hope the sun is shining in New Orleans, Archibald. I hope there is respite in Mother Nature's daily reminders of her omnipresence. I want to tell you it got better after you left ... but I can't quite be sure.

Yours always,

CB

NEW SUNS

Bonnefanten Museum, Maastricht, Netherlands

Kahlil Joseph's exhibition at the Bonnefanten Museum was the European premier of *New Suns*. His exhibition was remarkable—a myriad of interdisciplinary art telling the story of Black America. Film, live performance, installation, cartoon, light display and a room full of Rastafarians smoking weed. It was serendipitous that I, a burnt-out Black liberation activist camping in my parents' back room, would meet a man documenting the Black struggle.

Inspired by an Octavia Butler quote from her 1993 book *Parable of the Sower*, Kahlil Joseph's exhibition moved me in ways I didn't expect. Black art is so often a juxtaposition, an affront to the colonial, stark, white backdrop of the gallery. With *New Suns*, this oxymoron was extrapolated by the cobbled European streets, the tall Aryan people and my own memories of two years spent searching for Blackness in this town.

There is nothing new
under the sun,
but there are new suns.
—Octavia Butler

DEAR KAHLIL

I

Another mother-child outing landed us here. A seven-minute bike ride from the ugly 1960s brick structure my mother made beautiful. Painted family portraits, quirky market trinkets, salvaged wood my dad thought looked "friendly" and the mess of a good childhood.

I'd read a lot about the Dutch—a culture so close yet so different to my own. Us— Victorian, prudish, reserved. Them—liberated, equal, collective. They are by no means free of racism—a colonial nation is always a colonial nation. The wafting smell of satay or the ever-presence of Afrikaners are a reminder of the past. But the constant and real fear of total annihilation that lies in the combination of the choppy Atlantic Ocean and an abundance of land below sea level culminates in centuries of the universe's most effective teamwork. It's a simplified conclusion, but I wonder if the threat of complete geological destruction is the answer to world peace.

My desire for liberation is so simultaneously intense and hopeless that I'm relying on a meteor to save us.

Kahlil, I knew of you as the director of Beyoncé's Lemonade, *and that was all I needed to get me on my bike on the rainy evening you were in town. My mother and I cycled from Heugem, the sleepy conservative village we somehow called home, to the Bonnefanten Museum, a looming structure shaped like a bullet on the banks of the Maas.*

II

you are the shyest artist I've ever met
lips pursed, head bowed, arms folded, when I meet you

maybe,
you, like I, have been wounded
trying to find respite

you the artist,
me the activist

maybe,
like me, your life's work is searching for Black joy
and
drowning in Black pain

Yours always,
CB

NEW HORIZONS

I'm waiting for the new suns
Do they rise above new horizons?
Spill gold onto new waves
(boats of black bodies ebbing to unwanting shores)
Do they photosynthesize new plants?
Make new life
For a Black liberation

Can we start over? If we have new suns?
Can we flood the earth?
Make new babies the colour of soil
Rewrite stories that wrote us into the dirt
Can we captain the ships, this time?
Can we sow seeds that will grow into fruits of revolution?

I'm waiting for new suns
New dawns, new days, new light
that casts shadows only to keep us cool
that makes melanin, loves melanin

New moons, maybe
for new nights
new dreams

BLACK MEN DON'T RIDE HORSES

I don't quite remember
when my heart broke for the last time
I stopped attending vigils
because I ate grief for breakfast

SALT.

PuSh Festival, Vancouver, Canada

Slavery is a piece of colonial history that exists as connective tissue between all Black bodies, past, present and future. In *salt.*, Selina Thompson artistically narrates her own endeavour to retrace the theft of our collective ancestors via ship. In her one-woman show, Thompson evokes rage, despair, hatred and gratitude all at once.

As with any show in the depths of a Canadian January, the theatre was filled with cold and gloomy people. Mostly white, mostly people who use the word "culture" to refer to theatre. Thompson, whose accent and body and rage looked and sounded exactly like my own, chronicled the violence of the transatlantic slave trade with a rock of salt, a sledgehammer and the pain of a body weighted down by intergenerational memory.

DEAR SELINA

We shuffled in, anxious, exhausted, raging. We brought with us the weight of our days, the anti-Blackness, the fatphobia, the misogyny that had plagued us since sunrise. We wanted nothing more than to collapse, to lie under the weight of it all. To let it bleed out into our bedsheets, to let it wash away into slumber. But instead we dragged our bodies here. Into a space filled with white walls, white people and white noise.

Us: hopeful, expectant, fearful, outsider.

Them: curious, fascinated, guilty, fragile.

The seats were black, hard, portentous in their rows, and you stood there, Black resilience draped in white. And I stood there, too—butt hovering above the fold-down seat— awe stretching across my body.

Just then, in that moment, as you stood ominously before us, you were everything I believed we could become. I knew, without a glimpse of your show's content, you would tell me the story I've always been waiting to hear.

As if carved from marble, the Grecian gown folded around your body. A body like mine. A body unlike theirs. A body that turns heads in this town.

You said you took a boat—retracing, in some ways, parts of a passage our ancestors took, though through time, luck, strife and resilience, the boat you took was voluntary.

Under the dim lights, I felt the vibrations of white people. Consumed by an intergenerational fascination with you/me/us. Enraged at their ancestors and counterparts—but never at themselves. Oblivious, mostly, to their complicity in the story you tell.

I also felt the Black bodies—some were my friends; others were people I wished I knew. Most were tense, leaning forward, metaphorical arms outstretched to hold you or be you or something else.

You pounded rocks of salt into powder—a metaphor for the anti-Blackness imposed by state/corporation/man/fellow negro. You told a story—raw, intimate, oscillating, malignant —and I felt your body breaking.

Tears seated themselves in my lower lids. I felt a strange churning in my chest. It was pain and angst and longing and love and hurt ... and jealousy. Everything I know of West Africa and the Caribbean, the places you travelled to retrace our ancestors' fatal voyage, is from books and pictures and distant childhood memories. I yearn for the trauma of your journey, so I can experience the enlightenment that awaits on the other side.

After the show, a line formed and you sat handing out pieces of the crumbled salt to eager Vancouverites. I wanted to push past all of the white people and claim your time for myself. I wanted to take all of the salt hunks and build us a palace. Would it cost you more emotional labour to smile at all of them or to spend thirty minutes easing the pain they caused me?

A few months later, your work is still emanant in my body. A white lady sits across from me at dinner. "I still have that piece of salt," she says. I think of all the other broken things that made her home, too.

Yours always,

CB

CHILD

"FATHER"

on my eighteenth birthday, you sent me a package
for once, he has remembered my birthday
inside, I found everything I ever gifted you, returned to me

the pain, I think, was in my mother's tears
you didn't know he would turn out like this
in choosing to want me, Mama, you gave me everything

on a note, you wrote
"remember, child, blood is thicker than water"

now, on my Moon Days, I think of the indomitable strength of women and their wombs
of the thickness of blood
the cellular memory of trauma
ache betwixt my cervix

I also think of ocean,
of friendship, gifted companionship, requited and deserved admiration
of freshwater stream, mountain creek, rapids
of burning, bruising desire, of steaming, gushing, unfettered love

yes, blood is thick,

but
water
is
life

FIRST GRADE

the teacher told us to draw a self-portrait
I took the brown pencil and made lines across the paper
I kept inside the lines

"what's with the brown?" the teacher asked
and before I could say
it's the colour of me
her lip curled at the corner
she spoke the words into my face:

"you should try harder to wash off the mud"

twenty years have passed and I'm still trying
to wash off the dirt

THIRD GRADE

in third grade

a boy made all the girls line up facing the wall

the pain was not in the boys laughing

it was that the girls laughed

too

how hilarious it was that my body had developed too fast for the seams of my uniform

how wild it was that the line of my back was interrupted

how ugly it was that my body held shape, that I was not amorphous

how weird it was that Mama Africa gave me hips before I needed them

how do you defend a body it will take you twenty-five years to love?

FIFTH GRADE

an ugly white boy
called me a stupid nigger

teacher, teacher!

teacher crouched down
ironed chinos crinkling
aging back cracking
until he was eye level with me

"well, you're not stupid ..."

SEPARATION

I

around five I lay on my bed
a new one with a slide to the ground
back when mornings were exciting

I think a pillow or stuffed toy fell on my hand
I dreamed that both my parents were holding it
their fingers and palms touching each other's
and then mine

in that pregnant mid-wake slumber
where mosquitos sound like torpedoes
and flies become helicopters
the alarm clock is music, a soundtrack

there,

I am sure

my mother and father

my two parents

pressed their hands into each other's

and into mine

a promise of foreverness

a commitment to unconditional love

a dedication to be

my parents

when I woke up

there was only

one

II

one is more than enough

BOYS

boys learn violence

                                           before love

DEAR DIASPORA CHILD

it's okay if you only learned about your culture from Google

it's okay if you only read your language at the public library

it's okay if you need books to know your ancestral recipes

it's okay if you've never even set foot on the soil of your people

it's okay if your hips don't sway to those rhythms

it's okay if the food is too bitter for your tongue

it's okay if English is the only language that flows freely from your mouth

it's okay if your wardrobe is just jeans and Ts

it's okay if you only know Shakespeare

it's okay if spice brings you fear instead of joy

it's okay if you understand but can't reply

it's okay if you dread the disappointed stares of aunties

it's okay if small words like Salaam alaykum fall from your tongue like broken bones

it's okay if you spent your whole life shunning it all, only to now want it back

you are no less worthy
it is no less home

Love always,
CB

GENTRIFICATION OF MY HEART

my hometown oscillates between 1945 and the present

some days, she is modern, complex, moving
other days, she is still, silent, ravaged

my grandmother lives life like it's wartime
the sewing kit in the biscuit tin
a lifetime of rations in the pantry
a reuse mentality before it was cool
her home is a sanctuary of preservation

outside, condos replace childhood memories
an interior design store where the swings used to be

my heart begins to forget
the feeling of home

1942

Porthkerry Avenue
dimly lit, cool, barely breathing
her pavements a tendril of London,
stretching (hopelessly) towards an even colder sea

3 bedrooms
6 humans

walls expanding with love
remnants of a swing set creak in the garden
ghosts of celebration litter the stone pathway

she is small and round
blue eyes
travelling through mischief/fear/sorrow/wondering

a wail so violent
you can almost see it rippled across the grey sky

she gathers what she knows will keep her safe
Aloysius, the honey brown bear
Jane Eyre
rhubarb and custard hard-boiled sweets

a bellowing and angry vibration
rips through the aluminium frame
the family sit huddled, clutching sacred sentiments

is this it? is this the last time?

another rumble echoes dangerously
the babies cry

"mummy, was that a bomb?"

"no, that one was my fart."

1971

the wallpaper is brown as her skin
rotating in hues of orange—concentric circles,
hugging one another
a blotchy banana lies on the table
a blue grandfather chair looks on

garden shears lie hopelessly
in the grass
rough kinks of hair
forgotten, different, flat

once erect—shifting rigidly in the spring breeze
defiant,
rusty copper under sunshine

now, markedly lifeless
sleeping among dandelions

3 bedrooms
3 humans

she's learning how to be Black

and

white

in a time when there is mostly sepia

1981

this time her hair is straight

-ish

1999

they bury my dog
beneath the shrubs at the bottom of the garden

3 bedrooms
1 human

a tall-backed baby-blue chair,
silver paisley pattern slivers through its seams,
looks on from the corner

the old man from next door is in front of my face
his weighty, unrooted eye sockets come alive before me

the dog is dead
what?
the dog is dead
what?
the dog is dead

the old man from next door will also soon be dead.

STEP ON A CRACK, BREAK YOUR BACK

I was fifteen the first time I looked up

I had memorized the cracks in the pavement
like Bible passages

I would walk—

one foot in front of the other
head down
spine beginning to curve the wrong way
eyes trained half a metre in front
calves aching with tension

so focused on being invisible
I forgot how to see at all

UNAPOLOGETICALLY QUEER

I

queer desire was burning a hole in my chest pocket

I don't know how to live a half-life
I am not radioactive decay, atomic instability

it would be two hundred years short of my potential

I had to teach myself
how to love,
unapologetically
to exist,
in spaces that weren't ready for
my reverberating heart

II

I would be years late to realizing
half the people I loved had walked
out on me
because I'm queer

DEAR PETER

I never expected you.

Few people bring softness to my mother, and you did so with ease
You teased joy from the timid hearts of nervous first-years
You made concrete phallic structures seem like they could be home

·A heart so fierce, a smile so visceral, a hug so binding.
A joy so searing my fingertips burned at the thought of you.
I never expected to feel your laugh in my own chest.

I never expected to witness you
cradling a thousand hearts with the gentle grasp of a peach farmer
coaxing sunlight into cobwebbed corners
unfolding trauma, gently
building, building, growing, building
healing
inventing and reinventing intellectual intimacy
existing in forbidden ways
accidentally decolonizing
Fucking Shit Up

I never expected you

I expected loneliness
searching
trepidation
homesickness

Many of my university days were cold, lonesome ones—the campus stretched out like the silk lining of a coffin, soft and suffocating—the temptation to give in to them lay on the corner of every manicured lawn.

I missed everything. I missed all of the quiet and unnoticed ways my parents held me, created a container of love around me, made it so my life was entirely encased in ease.

Leaving home is a jarring experience, one of loss and uncertainty. You realize, the first time you make a doctor's appointment or do your own laundry, how truly lucky you were. Before long, the once-craved-for independence is the most terrifying thing you've ever had.

I yearn to be parented again. To be guided through cruel and unjust systems. To find heated waffles on my bedside table or lunch already stowed away in my backpack.

I found it all again, in you. I never expected a guardian. I never expected your gentle Blackness, your delicate masculinity. You defied everything I knew about Black men—you felt safe. There was something so indomitable about your spirit—I never expected you to leave.

Your memorial was filled with transformed people.
Lost souls, found. Empty hearts, filled. Wandering spirits, guided.

We sat between totem poles carved from ancestral wisdom, the hall filled with the sobs of people who will truly never know another person like you.

Over a punctured connection I told my mother you'd gone
"the moment I met him, I knew you would be safe in his hands"
this will be your legacy

Peter, the man who was always late—gone too early.

Rest in power,
CB

EVERYTHING ON EARTH

My earliest queer memory is sitting on the corner of Abhirami's bed one day after school. She lived in a weird part of town: much farther than everyone else, where London became countryside gradually, and then all of a sudden. The bus ride there felt like independence. Her home was a diaspora medley: smells and fabrics of Sri Lanka, two generations of the same family with vastly different ideas of home.

I don't remember much about Abhi's grade eight bedroom except that it felt temporary; she was a child accustomed to relocation. But I'll never forget the poster on the wall opposite her bed. It was vertical, a metre by a half, dark grey tones, a glossy sheen.

The poster depicted rain, like the same pathetic fallacy that fell outside the window that night. A black umbrella sheltered a woman from unnaturally torrential rain, and her body curved sideways, as though she actually wanted to get wet. In fact, when I looked closer, she already was wet—her white crop top had become transparent and her brown skin dripped with dewy Photoshopped raindrops.

She was Rihanna. And I was definitely gay.

I wonder often why I didn't come out sooner. I was born into a family built to withstand injustice, to defy the norm—a white grandmother who became pregnant by an African man in 1966 and a mixed-race mother who resulted from forbidden love. I don't know all the stories of my DNA—every memory slips through tight British lips with over-shoulder glances and never at family gatherings—but I know that we came to exist in times and spaces that were not ready. My father shipped from the colonies aged six, my parents unmarried, my stepfather staunchly working class and orphaned too soon. There was no variation of myself my family would not accept. My family is constructed of humans bred to value acceptance above all else.

So why, after hours spent giggling on Abhi's bed, did I not rush home to tell my parents the good news: "Mum, D, Nana—I'm gay!"? Instead, I came out seven years later, with three thousand miles and a telephone between us.

My adolescence was spent feigning interest in boys, punctuated by feelings of despair at my unattractiveness (turns out it was the boys who were ugly). I wish so much that I had lived my queer truth the moment I saw Rihanna in glossy, sexy 2-D form. I wish I had felt free, honest, genuine. I beat myself up for the life I missed by hiding, for the disservice I did my reality. Sometimes I watch queer youth online or during Pride and when I should feel proud, happy for them ... I feel jealous.

I know that after they asked a few questions, my parents would have been my greatest champions; my friends would have carried on unfazed.

And yet.

Child of the Cool Mum; friend of kind, compassionate people; grandchild of an activist; student of a Western education; bearer of the freest passport; citizen of a "progressive" nation. All of the avenues for queer freedom were there.

And yet.

white supremacy organized religion christian imperialism my colonized ancestors non-secular government heteronormative narratives disney princesses expectations of girlhood gender binary if he pushes you he likes you kiss-chase my body that grew too fast.

It is not anything specific that silenced my queer truth.

It's everything on Earth.

THIS BODY

I've never given birth
but my stretch marks show this body holds the weight of a thousand lives

SPIRITUAL DYSPHORIA

my body is spiritual dysphoria
I walk between Islam and Christianity and nothingness
I sit on prayer mats and on pews and on rusting park benches

they call us witches
they call us faggots
I have been burned at stakes made from trees felled on stolen land

I hope I will find Paradise
between sheets made wet by angry and swollen love

I have learned to trust in chosen family and in forbidden desire
I must learn, also, to trust in chosen afterlife

they call us sinners
they call us queer

if we are in the business of reclamation
let's take back Heaven.

Artwork References

Kahlil Joseph, *m.A.A.d*, 2014

Kahlil Joseph, *The Philosopher*, 2017

Kahlil Joseph, *Wildcat (Aunt Janet)*, 2016

Kahlil Joseph, *Wizard of the Upper Amazon*, 2016

Carolyn Mims Lawrence, *Black Children Keep Your Spirits Free*, 1972

Archibald J. Motley Jr., *The First One Hundred Years: He Amongst You Who Is without Sin Shall Cast the First Stone: Forgive Them Father for They Know Not What They Do*, c. 1963–72

Faith Ringgold, *American People Series #20: Die*, 1967

Betye Saar, *The Liberation of Aunt Jemima*, 1972

Selina Thompson, *salt.*, 2016

Acknowledgments

There are so many people who helped bring *Burning Sugar* to life. Firstly, of course, my family, who both literally and metaphorically gave me the magical, rich and fortunate life I have. My mum, Antoinette Blain; my grandmother Jean Robertson; my stepfather, David Chessell; and my brother, Remy Chessell, have been my anchors from day one. They have instilled in me the importance of a happy life, a love for adventure, a deep sense of justice and, most importantly, the knowledge that I can do whatever I put my mind to.

This process would not have been possible without the eminent Vivek Shraya, who believed my work was worthy of her time and dedication. I am so grateful for the opportunity to be mentored by someone who is changing the Canadian arts and literary scene and still makes time for my anxious emails. Thank you also to the team at Arsenal Pulp Press, who made me feel supported and nurtured throughout the process. Shirarose Wilensky, Brian Lam, Jazmin Welch and Cynara Geissler—you are all superstars!

Thank you also to all my friends and chosen family in Vancouver, London and beyond, for all the late-night calls, motivational memes and feedback on my work. Shout out to the lit group chats—*Onion Ringlets, Janelle Lovers, braid bois, WoC Warriors* and *Flash Fryers*—thanks for the laughter that keeps me grounded.

I lost two loved ones during the writing of this book: my mentor Peter Wanyenya and my sweet little Nutmeg. In different ways their spirits have guided me to where I am now, and for that I am eternally grateful. Peter was truly like no other person I have met—genuinely selfless, kind and compassionate. His gentle, hilarious and caring soul has inspired me to be a better person, to believe in myself and to commit my life to justice and liberation, through my work and my words.

Photo by David Markwei

CICELY BELLE BLAIN is a Black/mixed, queer femme from London, now living on the lands of the Musqueam, Squamish and Tsleil-Waututh peoples. At the heart of their work, Cicely Belle harnesses their passion for justice, liberation and meaningful change via transformative education, always with laughter, and fearlessly, in the face of resistance. They are noted for founding Black Lives Matter Vancouver and subsequently being listed as one of *Vancouver* magazine's 50 most powerful people, *BCBusiness*'s 30 under 30 and the CBC's 150 Black women and non-binary people making change across Canada. They are now the CEO of Cicely Blain Consulting, a social justice–informed diversity and inclusion consulting company with more than 100 clients across North America, Europe, Asia and Africa. Cicely Belle is an instructor in executive leadership at Simon Fraser University, a board member for the PuSh International Performing Arts Festival and a dialogue associate at the Morris J. Wosk Centre for Dialogue. Cicely Belle loves dinosaurs, Instagram and YA fantasy.

@cicelybelle

#burningsugarbook